Silken Weave

A History of Ribbon Making in Coventry from 1700 to 1860

By
Jenny Dodge

Silken Weave
A History of Ribbon Making in Coventry from 1700 to 1860

The Herbert, Jordan Well, Coventry CV1 5QP

Written by Jenny Dodge

First published by the Herbert Art Gallery and Museum 1988
ISBN 1-85316-009-1

2nd Edition published by The Herbert 2007
ISBN 978-0-9541185-5-6

Preface

At the heart of the city of Coventry stand the slender spires of Holy Trinity Church and of the ruined Cathedral of St Michael. Their neighbouring parishes, largely flattened by slum clearance and wartime blitz, are covered by austere post-war building. Only the two churches, St Mary's Hall and a scatter of old houses remind us of how this area used to look and what purpose it served.

150 years ago these parishes were a tangle of narrow, cobbled streets, lined with timbered houses. Leading off these streets were alleys, courts and yards packed with cramped brick cottages. Here the Coventry artisan lived and worked. Men, women and children laboured in small workshops or topshops or simply in the family living room. Factory work came late to Coventry: until well after the mid 19th century, the majority of artisans worked at home, surrounded by their families.

Two trades dominated the city: one was watchmaking, the other the weaving of silk ribbon. For well over 160 years ribbon weaving produced much of the city's wealth. With the exception of the firm of Cash's, the trade has now vanished as completely as the homes of the weavers themselves. In Earl Street, Much Park Street, Gosford and Far Gosford Street, Jordan Well and in Hillfields and Foleshill the grind of traffic has replaced the clacking of the looms.

With so little tangible evidence remaining it is easy to see why Coventry's visitors and many of its inhabitants are unaware of the lost industry. Fortunately some samples of ribbon have survived, enough to demonstrate the quality of the product. With the help of these and of the few contemporary documents that have come down to us we can begin to piece together the history of the ribbon weavers of Coventry.

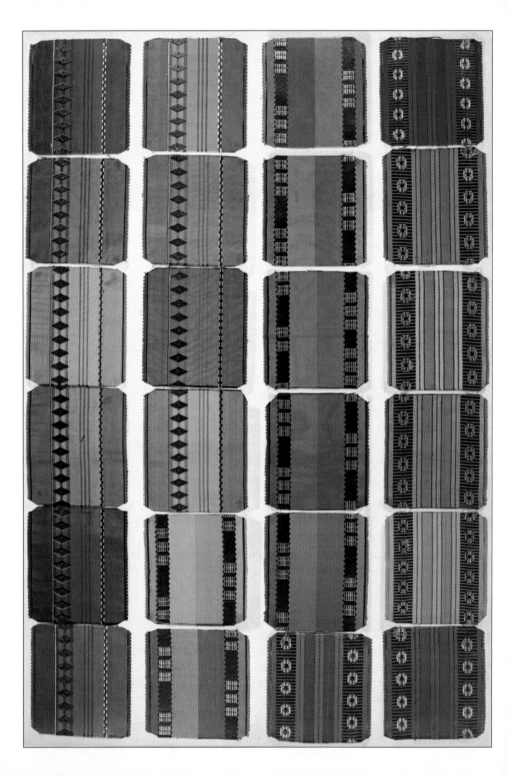

Contents

The Beginnings of the Trade

In 1703 a Mr Thomas Bird set up the first recorded silk ribbon weaving establishment in Coventry. However, he was drawing upon skills in weaving which had been part of the city's industrial heritage base since medieval times and was responding to changes in the economy which made this a viable prospect.

The ribbon trade brought prosperity to Coventry. The weavers of silk, formerly joined with the weavers of worsted, formed their own Company of Silk Weavers and marched yearly in the Godiva Procession under their own magnificent silk banners. More and more young people served their seven year apprenticeship in the trade and became journeymen weavers. The trade ran in families; children helped in the family workshop from an early age and were apprenticed to their father's trade at 13.

Ribbon woven to commemorate the coronation of George III in 1761.

Thomas Bird became a wealthy man and other silk merchants set up in Coventry. The 18th century saw the rise of the ribbon manufacturers: rich, paternalistic and few in number. They lived in great houses only a stone's throw from the humble homes of the weavers. Coventry people called them the Great Masters.

The Great Masters concerned themselves only with the buying in of raw silk from France and Italy and the delivery of finished ribbon to the retailer in London. The preparation of silk and the weaving of ribbons were carried out through middlemen known as undertakers. These men undertook to see the silk through the process of throwing, dyeing and weaving. They used local throwsters to clean the silk, boil it clean of gum and twist the long filaments into yarn. Organzine was the name given to the warp yarn which was used to dress the loom. It was given a hard twist and doubled for strength. Tram was the name for the weft, the yarn used to fill the shuttles. The thrown silk was then dyed to brilliant colours while in the hank. The warp and weft were given out to the weaver who wove a 'piece' of 36 yards working between two stains set on the warp by the undertaker. The ribbon manufacturer paid the undertaker according to the breadth and quality of the ribbon and the undertaker paid the weaver two thirds of the money.

Raw silk was expensive and silk was weighed at every stage of manufacture to guard against theft or the substitution of cheaper yarns, such as cotton. A fixed allowance was made for wastage during throwing and weaving. Even the finished ribbon was weighed and carefully checked before it was rushed off to London by coach. A weaver who wove a less than perfect piece had his money docked, a process he generally considered unfair.

The ribbon trade, protected after 1766 by an embargo on imported silk goods, flourished in Coventry. In 1782 a traveller, Thomas Pennant, wrote about it in his journal: 'It has extended to a great degree and is supposed to employ at least 10,000 people and has likewise spread into the neighbouring towns such as Nuneaton and other places. Such good results from our little vanities'.

The little vanities, purchased by the fashionable London lady, kept the weaver in work. Ribbons were an essential part of their dress, used to trim gowns and bonnets, to tie up hair for a ball and lace dainty shoes, for waistbands, sashes, frills, favours and rosettes. Small children were smothered in ribbon. Curtains and cushions were embellished with broad bands of shining silk. Ribbon was produced in an amazing variety of weaves and colours: plain, striped, checked, watered, shot, shaded and figured.

A Victorian dress decorated with ribbons.

A handloom still in use in 1919.

In the early days of the trade ribbon was woven on single handlooms. These produced one ribbon at a time. After 1770, the introduction of the Dutch engine loom, which despite its name, was hand operated, enabled the weaver to produce up to six ribbons simultaneously. Male weavers decided that this loom should be for their exclusive use and confined the female worker to the operation of the single handloom. However, since the engine looms were heavy to use and could produce plain ribbon only, the skilled female weaver might not have been concerned; by manipulating the warp with the fingers, the weaver could produce figured ribbon on her single hand loom and it was considered that the finest ribbon of all was woven on them. Good figured ribbon fetched a higher price than plain. Gradually the Dutch engine loom replaced the single handloom in the city though the latter continued to be widely used in the country districts.

'Looms upon different constructions are there,
Some made to weave silk and some woollens, some hair.
Good work to all weavers who tie well their ends in,
In broad looms, in narrow, likewise in the engine.'

(Sung in a Coventry theatre, 1781)

Throughout the 18th century more and more weavers set up their looms within the city of Coventry. The number of country weavers increased too, producing ribbon in Foleshill, Bedworth, Bulkington, Exhall, Nuneaton and in the small villages to the north of Coventry. Many of the female weavers were the wives of the colliers, weaving ribbon to supplement the family's income. Work was delivered to them through the undertaking system. It was said that a weaver would look for a wife who could weave and could earn good money. The city weaver preferred a country lass because she was bigger and healthier than a city girl.

Wives who did not weave were expected to assist by winding the weft silk by means of a wheel onto a quill of stiff paper to be inserted into the shuttle. Both the shuttle and the weft yarn were known as the shute. If there were children of six and over, they were made to fill the shute with the quill of silk, to run errands and help look after the younger children. All the family worked to enable the weaver to earn enough to provide for them.

The expanding trade led to a demand for more accommodation in the city. This led to a problem. The Coventry journeyman could become a Freeman of the city and, by ancient decree, was entitled to grazing rights on the commons surrounding the city wall. This meant that the land could not be used for new housing. From the mid 18th century onward the back gardens of the old timbered houses in the city were gradually in-filled with new houses, crammed into a maze of alleys, yards and courts. The ribbon manufacturer found that an unsanitary yard had grown up just over his garden wall. As soon as he could, the Great Master moved away from the city to a new villa well away from the town.

'What wonders every day we see, sirs,
In the streets of Coventry, sirs,
New roads, new lanes, new yards, new courts, sirs,
With new buildings of all sorts, sirs.
Where hedges, ditches, ponds of water,
Now there's nothing but bricks and mortar,
They will extend I do suppose, till
Coventry will reach to Foleshill!'

(Sung at the Old Theatre, Smithford Street,
early 19th century)

Changes in the Trade

The first major change in the structure of the ribbon trade in Coventry came with the Napoleonic Wars. Skilled weavers were recruited for the army, leaving the trade short of labour. The demand for silk ribbon was as high as ever and could not be met. Even the smuggling of vast quantities of French ribbon, almost an industry in coastal villages, was affected. To add to the difficulties, there was a sudden female clamour in fashionable England for a new design of ribbon with purl edges. The purl-edged ribbon was woven with horsehair edging to the warp; this was withdrawn from the woven ribbon, leaving attractive scallops on one or both sides of it. In 1813, the 'big purl time' came to Coventry and turned the trade upside down. Weavers were used to good and bad times but they had never known a time when the demand for their product was so fierce. In London, manufacturers could ask what prices they wished: every yard was sold and weavers revelled in prosperity. It was later said that an advertisement was placed by weavers in the local paper requesting the services of 50 poor watchmakers to come round on a Saturday night and shell peas for them!

The big purl time lasted until the middle of 1815. Then it died away as swiftly as it had come. Such are the vagaries of fashion. It left in its wake changes in the organisation of the trade. The Great Masters had been phasing out the undertaking system in the city by dealing direct with the weaver. Now the ribbon manufacturer saw to the preparation of the silk and the weaver collected warp yarn to dress the loom and weft in the hank for his wife to wind. He delivered the finished ribbon direct to the manufacturer. In a short time the city undertaker found himself without business. Many undertakers went bankrupt. Those who had managed to save a little capital bought some looms and set up loom-shops.

In the big purl time, when demand was at its peak, the new loom-shop owner, finding himself short of skilled weavers because of the war, changed the apprenticeship system to suit his needs. He invented the half-pay apprentice. He took into his employment boys and girls in their early teens and gave them a hasty training in the art of weaving. In about 18 months, he reckoned, he could turn them into adequate weavers.

They refunded him half their wages to pay for board and lodging and their training. To save himself money, the loom-shop owner employed a high percentage of female and child labour at a modest wage. They did winding and warping, picking-up (cleaning the warp at the back of the loom of knots and snags) and filled the shutes. Coventry folk gave the loom-shop owner a title. They called him the 'Little Master'.

In 1815 the war with France ended and the weavers returned to their looms. By this time, the big purl time was over and the trade was slack. The half-pay apprentice system had undermined the status of the journeyman weaver, a man who had served seven years as an apprentice and become a proud Freeman of the city, entitled to the franchise. But, worse than that, the returning journeyman found himself unable to earn enough to support his family.

The weaver and his family suffered great hardship, and in 1818 a Parliamentary Commission was set up to inquire into the changed condition of the Coventry trade. Expert witnesses, among them a Coventry ribbon manufacturer, and experienced journeyman weaver and a silk merchant from London gave evidence. The weaver, when asked how his earnings compared with former years of both good and bad, he replied 'They have never been lower than now'. Each of the witnesses agreed that the answer lay in a small rise in the retail price of ribbon: a farthing or so a yard. They felt that such an increase would not trouble the wealthy customer.

Unfortunately this simple solution did not prevail against market forces; the retailer could always find good supplies of cheaper ribbon. French ribbon was smuggled in enormous quantities and the Little Master undercut the Great Master by pirating his new designs and flooding the market. Seasonal manufacturers, known by the delightful name of 'Cuckoo Masters', cashed in on the high demand for ribbon in the spring when summer gowns and bonnets were trimmed. The price of raw imported silk fluctuated wildly. When the death of a Royal personage plunged the entire fashionable world into mourning, dark ribbon was the only acceptable trim to bonnets and dress. The entire season's production of coloured ribbon became unmarketable and had to be dumped.

A page from a sample book recording the death of Princess Amelia in 1810.

'I have determined to trim my lilac sarsenet with black satin ribbon. Ribbon trimmings are all the fashion at Bath.'

(In a letter home from Jane Austen, outlining her plans for adjusting her wardrobe following a death in the Royal Family).

The Coventry weaver struggled on, hoping for another big purl time. When the trade was good, he made a little profit, when it was bad he tightened his belt. The trade, which in the 18th century had promised a good living, was changing fast and the weaver had to manage as best he could.

After the 'big purl time'...

During the 1820s, the ribbon trade saw many changes. In the city many small loom-shops operated, employing journeymen, half-pay apprentices, women and children. The ribbon manufacturer now dealt directly with the journeyman weaver. It was this type of weaver who became known as the first-hand journeyman, the archetypal artisan ribbon weaver of 19th century Coventry. He was a businessman in his own right now that the undertaker had disappeared from the city trade and, however much he suffered in trade recessions, he retained his skills and his pride.

The Coventry census returns of 1841 and 1851 give us the names of the first-hand and his family and show us streets thickly inhabited with weavers. The apprenticeship rolls show us the young men who served their seven years and became journeymen and Freemen of Coventry. This is as close as we can get to the individual weaver of these years. With the exception of Joseph Gutteridge and, later, William Andrews, who wrote some account of their lives in the weaving community, no memories, no diaries or letters remain. But we know a little about how the weavers lived from parliamentary reports, health reports and newspapers.

The first-hand fetched home the warp and weft silk from the manufacturer, having contracted to deliver a piece of a particular breadth and weave. He dressed his loom with the warp while his wife, or a woman employed by him, wound the weft for the shute: his children filled the shute. The following Saturday, he delivered the finished ribbon to the manufacturer and took his money. This was called 'taking in the fell' and had a certain amount of ceremony attached to it. The weaver took a pride in his appearance and never visited the manufacturer without washing and shaving and donning a black tail-coat and a well brushed hat. He was acknowledged in the trade as a gentleman among artisans. After giving his wife her housekeeping and paying any debts, the first-hand retired to his local public house to meet his friends and drink a pint or two of ale.

Strikes and disputes

From time to time disputes with manufacturers over prices came to a head and the weavers would assemble in large numbers. Gosford Green was a favoured meeting place. The city area where the weavers lived was so small that it was said that one man with a hand-bell could walk round it and summon them to a meeting the same day. The usual demand of the weavers was for a fixed list of prices for producing ribbon but this the manufacturers were reluctant to give, owing to the fluctuations in the price of raw silk and the uncertainties of the market. A list might be drawn up (the first was in 1813 and others followed) and signed by the manufacturers. Some failed to keep to the list and some refused to sign. There were many meetings and demonstrations. The weavers had a rough way of dealing with a manufacturer who offended them; they placed the unfortunate man on a donkey, facing the tail, and paraded him through the streets. This was known as 'donkeying'.

Price lists were not all that concerned the weaver during these early years of the 19th century; the tide of industrial revolution was sweeping across Europe, bringing changes in machinery and working habits. It was difficult for the independent artisan to keep his head above water. Looms became bigger and heavier as mechanical improvements made it possible to weave greater numbers of ribbons simultaneously. This put physical strains on the weaver who spent long hours at the loom every day. The jacquard loom was introduced to Coventry in 1823 when we find a Mrs Dresser using one in her loom-shop. This loom, with its system of using punched cards to control the lifting of individual warp threads, made possible the production of figured ribbon on a larger scale than before. Not only could it weave more ribbons than a single handloom but the designs were more intricate. The product was in great demand in the fashionable world. In 1823 there were five jacquard looms in Coventry; in 1826 there were 209.

A jacquard loom, built in 1845. This loom is in The Herbert's collections.

The buying of a large, sophisticated loom was beyond the means of many weavers and those who managed to invest in one often had to break through the upper floors of their little houses to accommodate the superstructure. Bigger and heavier still was the à la bar loom. The weaver could now weave, using hand-power, a quantity of ribbons simultaneously. But this increased productivity had its drawbacks. Not only was the health of the new weaver affected by the strains being placed on his back and chest but he needed more assistance in preparing wound silk, filling the shute and cleaning the silk in the loom. If his family were not able to help him, he had to pay for labour. The heaviest looms needed a loom turner to help the weaver lift the shafts. This was usually a young lad.

In spite of disputes and uncertainties in the trade, the Coventry first-hand held his own during the 1820s and 1830s and the fortunate ones prospered. In 1826 an area of land outside the city became available for building and the Hillfields district was established with dwellings constructed to accommodate the first-hand journeyman and his family. Here were two and three storey brick houses with built-in topshops, which suited the better off weaver who might own two or three looms and take in apprentices. He might also rent a loom to a second-hand journeyman and have female employees to wind silk and pick up behind the loom.

In 1832 a new challenge to the handloom weavers appeared. Josiah Beck, a mechanic, set up a factory in St Agnes Lane in the city and filled it with steam-powered looms. A furious mob of weavers invaded the factory, cut the silk from the looms and threw it into the river. The factory was set on fire and the looms broken into pieces. The unfortunate Mr Beck escaped by scrambling over the back wall. The old St Michael's parish hand-engine was quite unable to put out the fire and the factory burnt to the ground. Arrests followed and the ringleaders were sentenced to hang but, after appeals by the local Member of Parliament, the sentences were commuted to transportation.

After this unhappy event, the introduction of steam power was delayed in Coventry until the late 1830s. Elsewhere, at Congleton, Derby and Leek, steam-powered looms wove ribbon from 1835 onwards and became a threat to Coventry trade even though, at this early stage, they wove only plain black ribbon. The handloom weaver, accustomed to regard himself as a skilled artisan, saw steam power as a threat to his livelihood and his craft. Harriet Martineau, visiting Coventry in 1851, commented, 'No place has made a more desperate resistance to the introduction of steam power'. By 1840, however, steam power had arrived in Coventry.

The Lives of the Ribbon Weavers

1840 is a good date at which to break off and examine what we know about the everyday life of the weaver.

In 1838, Joseph Fletcher visited Coventry to write a report on conditions in the Ribbon Trade for the Assistant Handloom Weavers' Commissioners. This report was presented to Parliament in 1840. The following pages are based on his report and on information found in the reports of Medical Officers of Health.

At the top of the trade, the 'gentleman among artisans', was the first-hand journeyman. The prosperous one was likely to be found residing in the newly built Hillfields district, with its streets named respectfully after members of the Royal family. He had a neat brick dwelling complete with a topshop where he and his family worked. His home was comfortably furnished with beds and drawers and, perhaps, a clock and kept generally neat and clean. His family lived on a plain but adequate diet of bread, vegetables, puddings and some meat and bacon. He could afford the extras: tea or coffee, milk, sugar, a glass or two of ale and a pipe at the local public house of an evening. His wife might wind a little silk or he might pay a woman to do it. He owned a patch of garden in which to grow vegetables, keep pigeons or fatten a pig in the sty. He was a man who had providently saved up for a loom of his own, who had rented out looms to a journeyman less well off than himself and was able to take on apprentices.

The weaver in the city parishes, crowded into rented accommodation in the streets and yards, was not so prosperous. He might own his own loom, or he might have to rent one. He was dependent on his family to provide unpaid labour to keep his loom filled with silk. His wife wound silk and his children filled the shute. The old timbered houses, sublet to several families, were crumbling and the new brick cottages in the courts and yards were 'small, dark and ill-ventilated'. They were also chilly. The weaver, working in his living room, had to keep the fire low or even put it out altogether in order to keep the silk at the right humidity and free from smoke and dirt. Streets were undrained and often ran with water; alleys and courts were filthy and unpaved. There was no sewage disposal or collection of refuse. The common privy-pit could be sited within a yard or two of a front door and heaps of rubbish and dung accumulated until it was worth somebody's while to cart it away. Visitors to Coventry remarked upon its 'intolerable stench'. Joseph Fletcher examined in his report the home of a typical city weaver, David Bradbury, who lived in 'two small rooms and a shop above'.

In these dark little houses, children were born and the lucky ones survived. The infant death rate was high, not surprising due to the fact that Coventry had a high rate of infant diarrhoea. Nevertheless, some of the families found in the 1841 census return for Gosford and Much Park Streets, numbered six or even eight growing children.

A court in Coventry.

As a result of the health reports the city began to improve its water supplies and refuse disposal and to cobble and drain the streets. But this took some years to do, and reports continued to come in from Medical Officers of foul middens, open ditches acting as sewers and privy pits in proximity to wells.

The city families did not eat as well as the families at Hillfields. There was little meat and few puddings. Bread and dripping or treacle and boiled potatoes with tea and a little milk and sugar provided the basic diet for adults and growing children alike.

Worst off of all was the country weaver who was still working at a single handloom. His cottage might be bare of all but a stool, table, old chair and a loom. There was not much bedding and often no bedstead at all. Young married couples frequently could not afford to rent a home and lived apart, in lodgings. Since the young women 'kept company' from an early age and sometimes did not marry until far gone in pregnancy, the sufferings of young families must have been extreme.

For those who could not scrape a living there was parish relief and the workhouse. The weaver dreaded the times of bad trade in case he was forced onto the parish. This would deprive him of his rights as a Freeman and of his right to vote. The well-to-do and the clergy of Coventry who understood his plight, organised private charities and soup kitchens when times were bad but were powerless to provide the weaver with the one thing he really needed: the means of earning his own living.

Education and Leisure

In the 1851 census returns for the city, it is surprising to see so many weavers' children described as 'scholar'. Even children of two are listed in this way and most boys and girls up to the age of eight. But a rosy picture of the children of artisans receiving education is a little dimmed by the revelations in Fletcher's report that most weavers' children went to 'out-of-the-way schools'. This was the local nickname for a dame school and reveals the sad truth that the children were sent there to get them out of the way while parents worked at home. These tiny schools were run by poor widows trying to scratch a living, and housed in kitchens, 'low and confined'; dirty, dark and barely 12 feet square. The dames, who often knew no more than the alphabet themselves, were unable to instruct children in reading and writing. Many of the children were tiny, attending with a 'nurse-girl' to look after them. There were a few tattered books to look at, a stinking yard or alley to play in. The little schoolroom doubled as a shop, selling needles and pins, tape and apples. The children left at the age of eight, knowing little catechism and one or two hymns. For this education the parents paid two pence a week for each child.

There were also charity schools in Coventry, such as Bablake and Fairfax's Charity and the National and Lancasterian Schools, which would provide a better education for the artisan's child. Doubtless some of the more fortunate attended them. Nevertheless the weaver required the services of every child from eight upwards and from that age the child became one of the family workforce.

Country children had only Sunday school to go to. These were sectarian, used mainly for religious inculcation and run by voluntary teachers, some barely literate.

Efforts were made from the 1830s onward to provide education for the adult artisan in Coventry. The chapels of Cow Lane and Vicar Lane ran a book society with a library, 'comprised chiefly of religious, biographical and historical works, and books of voyages, travels and missions'.

Book sellers lent books at two pence a time and the Mechanics' Institute, established in 1828, had a library, reading room, laboratory and classroom where the working man might learn writing, arithmetic, geometry, geography and grammar at a cost of two shillings and sixpence a quarter. The cost was a little high for the family man but young weavers attended. There is no mention of female students.

The weaver worked long hours, whether in factory, loom-shop or at home and his leisure was precious to him. If he was not tending a garden or drinking in the public house, he might well saunter with his friends on the common land that surrounded the city. We are told that the weaver was fond of nature study and the commons were a natural habitat for many species of plants and insects, birds and animals. The weaver and his family, crammed into dark rooms all the week, must have found this place a paradise. Joseph Gutteridge recalls many happy hours spent on the commons as a boy and young man. Primrose Hill in those days was smothered with blossoms in the spring.

The public house to the weaver was more than a place to drink and smoke. There was a sense of fraternity among the weavers and the public house was the place where they discussed manufacturers' prices, politics and their favourite pastimes of gardening, pigeon fancying, canary breeding and boxing. They ran their benefit clubs there too, often asking the landlord to hold the money on their behalf. All money paid in and out of the clubs, whether for sickness or burial, was done over the table in the bar. This was not entirely a male pastime; women weavers and silk workers ran benefit clubs of their own, also in public houses, as a visitor to Coventry in the 1830s severely observed: 'They are exposed to…temptations against which their frailty is not proof '. Sometimes political life and feasting were combined; in the early 1860s the local press recorded a famous political speaker holding forth in the backyard of a popular pub and the roasting whole of a sheep in celebration of the event. The womenfolk, it seems, were assigned a room to themselves where they feasted upon sausages and tripe.

The leisure pursuits of the country weaver were not, according to Joseph Fletcher, as decorous as those of the city weaver. At Foleshill, the inhabitants were notorious for drinking, bastardy, thieving and ignorance and were addicted to robbing the barges moored on the Grand Junction canal. At Bulkington the lads stole chickens, ducks, geese, turkeys and sheep. They even pulled up 'the pet vegetables of the respectable inhabitants to whom they knew their proceedings to be obnoxious'.

Worst of all was 'Black Bedworth', (as Fletcher called it) where there was bull-baiting, drunkenness, brawling and cock-fighting and the women stripped to fight in the street. Generally the country weaver was seen as a barbarian; unwashed, non-church going and without a clean shirt till Monday. We are told, however, that the women were neighbourly and sent their children to Sunday school.

When times were good, the Coventry weaver and his family managed well enough. Yet the days when a man or woman could make a living at hand weaving were fast drawing to a close. Steam power was well established in other weaving towns and the time had come when Coventry must accept it or go under.

Steam Power and Factories

During the 1840s and 1850s the factories and mills were built, first on a small scale, then bigger and bigger, employing many silk workers. These all made use of steam-powered looms. It would be tempting to assume that the Industrial Revolution had now reached Coventry and that factory working took over from the traditional out-working in the ribbon trade. In fact this was not the case: the situation was far more complex. Ribbons were now produced on steam-powered looms in factories, on hand-powered looms of various sizes in homes and topshops, and also in loom-shops. Silk workers might be factory employees, loom-shop employees, loom renters or second-hands, first-hands and their families or employees. In the city, the odd single handloom weaver remained, possibly a widow or old man. Country weavers still used the single handloom and the old undertaking system continued to operate in Bedworth, in Exhall and in the colliery villages.

By the end of the 1840s, half of the working population of Coventry was in the ribbon trade. In 1851, out of a total population of 22,365, the silk workers numbered 10,641. In the 30 or so mills there were 1,000 power looms and 2,000 workers. Nevertheless, four out of five workers in the ribbon trade were outdoor workers. It must be admitted that the productivity of the steam-powered looms was higher than that of any hand-powered loom yet they were not always able to weave the high quality ribbon produced on a handloom.

After the trade embargo on foreign silk goods was lifted in 1824, the competition in the top fashion trade became intense and the factories of Coventry found a convenient middle and lower-class market for their goods. Prosperity in England was increasing and there was a little over from the housekeeping to indulge in a small piece of ribbon to trim a bonnet or a bridal gown for a working girl. The first-hand with his handloom could weave a high quality ribbon, plain or figured, which would fetch a higher price per piece but found that he had to work very hard to keep up with the competition from the French ribbon, flooding into London shops. Some manufacturers thought that English ladies bought French ribbons because of their superiority in design, but one manufacturer grumbled, 'they buy them because they are French'.

There was now a new type of ribbon weaver in Coventry, the factory worker. Hitherto the weaver had been able to fix his own working hours and had enjoyed this freedom. Now he or she was tied to the factory hours dictated by the running of the steam engine. Pay was docked for lateness and the foremen ruthlessly enforced factory rules. By tradition the weaver had worked hard during the week until he finished his piece, often labouring into the night on a Friday. He delivered his work on a Saturday and then had Sunday off usually for his enjoyment as he was not always a great church-goer. The following day he observed as 'St Monday' and had an extra day's holiday. He started work somewhat late on Tuesday morning. Factory wages were adequate and regular but the weaver still had to produce ribbon of set lengths and good quality before receiving any pay.

The oldest surviving former ribbon factory in Coventry.

Factories continued to invest in larger, more productive looms and used cheap female labour. Now the weaver, who had considered himself a craftsman was used simply as a loom-minder, often running between mechanically operated shuttles while the picking-up was done by a woman standing at the back of the loom. Little wonder that the factory worker often suffered from headaches, insomnia and nosebleeds! The female workers, employed at winding, warping or picking up had to work as long hours for far less pay. The pickers-up stood all day behind the loom. Married women worked in these factories, as well as young single girls, often throughout the full term of pregnancy. After giving birth, they returned to the factory, sometimes within a couple of weeks. A local Medical Officer reported in 1856 that factory women could be seen 'at an early hour on their way to the mills, with their children only half-dressed, carrying the remainder of their clothes and their food for the day, to be left with the person who had charge of the child during its mother's absence, and this oft-times on a cold winter's morning in the midst of sleet or snow'.

In an attempt to keep up with competition the first-hand journeyman began to turn to steam power. Neighbouring weavers joined together to rent an engine, which they installed in a street or yard, running shafts from it through their own houses to power their looms. One old Coventry man remembered years later how, as a small boy, he had lain in bed and watched the shaft turning above his head. The noise and vibration could not have been pleasant for weavers' families and, worst of all, as soon as the engine was started in the morning, everyone had to start working. The old days of flexible working hours and St Monday were fast vanishing.

Design

In spite of troubles in the trade, there were those who still saw hope for the weavers. In 1851, a piece of broad silk ribbon, beautifully figured with flowers of varying hue was sent to the Great Exhibition and was much admired by the public and experts alike. This design is known as the Coventry Ribbon and there are samples of it in The Herbert. English designers were providing excellent patterns for ribbon by this time and schools of Art and Design were established.

The Coventry Ribbon woven for the Great Exhibition, 1851.

Ribbon manufacturers had been pressing for the training of good English designers for years and the Coventry School of Design was opened in a former warehouse in St John's Bridges in 1843. In 1863 it became the School of Art and was housed in a handsome new building. William Andrews trained in Coventry and won many a silver medal for his designs. In early years the English manufacturer had copied designs from French ribbons but now England was producing her own ribbon designers.

The School of Art, Ford Street, 1867.

Cottage Factories

Late in the 1840s a few liberal-thinking ribbon manufacturers came up with a new idea to help the first-hand make a living. Eli Green built the first cottage factory in Hillfields, with weavers' houses surrounding a three-sided yard. This became known as the Triangle. J and J Cash and other manufacturers followed his lead and other cottage factories were built. The idea was that one engine in a yard would power looms in the top-shops of the surrounding houses. The houses would be provided with good gardens where the weaver could grow vegetables for his family.

There was an idealistic philosophy attached to this business venture: the artisan could now benefit from new technology and, at the same time, retain the independence of a craftsman and a sturdy English peasant. The cottage factories were soon filled with weaving families and working busily. Whether this venture would have managed to save the Coventry first-hand from the decay that was creeping into the outwork system, it is impossible to say.

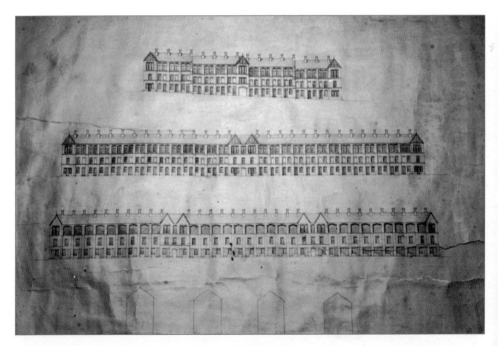

Architect's drawing of Cash's cottage factory at Kingfield, 1857.

The Cobden Treaty and After

By 1851 many of the names well known in the world of Coventry ribbon had become established. Some, such as John and Joseph Cash, started in a small way and have survived to this day, though their product is no longer silk ribbon. Other familiar names are Caldicott, Odell, Cope Hammerton and Franklin. The names number well over 100. Some manufacturers, like Mr Hart of Victoria Mill, employed hundreds of workers. Harriet Martineau visited such a mill in 1851 when she wrote her vivid descriptive article for Household Words. She entitled it 'Rainbow Making' and this quotation from it shows why:

'There were bride-like white-figured ribbons and narrow black, flimsy ones…There were checked ribbons of all colours and sizes in the check. There were stripes of all variety, width and hue. There were diced ribbons and speckled and frosted. There were edges which may introduce a wonderful harmony of colouring; as primrose with a lilac edge; green with a purple edge; rose colour and brown; puce and amber; and so on….'.

Previously she had visited a dye-works and seen 'bundles of glossy silk, or the most brilliant colours. Blues, rose-colours, greens, lilacs, make a rainbow of the place'.

In 1860 the Prime Minister, William Gladstone, dealt a major blow to the English silk trade and to the Coventry trade in particular. He signed the Cobden Treaty with France. The treaty removed tariffs from imported silk goods and, at the same time, made it more difficult for English manufacturers to export goods to the continent. Reportedly he answered his critics by indicating that he regarded the English silk trade as of little importance. It was a piece of irony that the Coventry Freemen, many of whom were weavers, had, by tradition, always voted for the Liberal Party and free trade. There had been many bad years, demonstrations over list breaking, strikes, riots, lock-outs and bankruptcies but never anything quite so devastating to the trade as one firm after another went out of business. Weavers and their families had to accept parish relief in spite of the soup kitchens and charities set up in Coventry to save them. Looms were broken up and the wood and iron that constructed them sold as scrap.

The weaver, Joseph Gutteridge, wrote of this time: 'Such a general state of extreme poverty was never known in Coventry before. Many weavers with large families were compelled to make raids upon the field camps of turnips and potatoes to save their children from utter starvation. The Workhouse was filled to overflowing; the rates went up enormously to supply the outdoor poor with a

A soup kitchen set up in St Mary's Hall to feed unemployed weavers and their families in 1861. *Illustrated London News*

scanty pittance: shopkeepers were on the verge of ruin and no credit could be obtained for food: the manufacturers one after another were going into bankruptcy and nearly 800 houses were soon without tenants. Hundreds of families emigrated by means of help to America and the colonies, and at home, besides the relief work on the Commons, soup kitchens were opened to appease the famished people who could get no bread'.

The slump lasted for several years, but was by no means the end of the ribbon trade. Some firms and some weavers survived the disaster and the old ribbon trade got through by diversifying its product. Manufacturers adapted looms to weave fringing, braid and elastic. Silk pictures remained a reliable product and many weavers took to weaving them. They produced bookmarks and fancy braids, medal ribbons and tapes. There was still ribbon produced and, from time to time during the late nineteenth century, the market boomed.

But the weaving of ribbons, plain and fancy was no longer a major industry in Coventry. Perhaps we should remember the words of one exasperated Coventry ribbon manufacturer reported in the Coventry Herald, 1859: 'Of all the risky, anxious trades the fancy ribbon trade is the most so. There is no gambling on the Stock Exchange, or even the turf, that is equal to it'.

Bibliography

The Victoria History of the County of Warwick, Volume Eight 1969

B. Poole, Coventry: Its History and Antiquities 1870

H. Jones, Still Weaving: J and J Cash Ltd of Coventry (The Herbert) 1998

H. Miles, The Coventry Silk Ribbon Industry from the Introduction of the use of the Dutch engine loom (c1770) to the Cobden Treaty (Unpublished B Litt, University of Oxford) 1930

J. Prest, The Industrial Revolution in Coventry 1960

P. Searby, Weavers and Freemen in Coventry, 1820-1861: social and political traditionalism in an early Victorian town (Unpublished Ph D thesis, University of Warwick) 1972

N. Tiratsoo, Coventry's Ribbon Trade in the mid-Victorian period; some social and economic responses to industrial development and decay (Unpublished Ph D thesis, University of London) 1980

F. Warner, The Silk Industry of the United Kingdom 1921

Minutes of the Evidence taken before the Committee appointed to consider of the several petitions relating to the ribbon weavers   1818

Joseph Fletcher, Report on the Midland Districts of England for the Assistant Hand-Loom Weavers' Commissioners Presented to the Houses of Parliament 1840

Joseph Gutteridge, Lights and Shadows in the Life of an Artisan, Coventry Free Press 1891

William Andrews, The Diary of William Andrews (unpublished)

Abridged versions of both of the above are published as Master and Artisan in Victorian England, ed. Valerie E. Chancellor; Evelyn, Adams & Mackay 1969

A. Heap, Newscuttings of the Nineteenth Century (Coventry and Warwickshire Collection)

Coventry Newscuttings of the Nineteenth Century (Coventry and Warwickshire Collection)

The Journal of Design and Manufacturers 1849-50

Harriet Martineau, 'Rainbow Making', Household Words 14 February 1852

The Silk Ribbon Collection at The Herbert

The Herbert is extremely fortunate in possessing a unique and beautiful collection of material relating to the silk weaving industry in Coventry. In addition to a vast collection of silk pictures (or 'Stevengraphs') the museum holds over 200 sample, design and pattern books; dyers' samples; documents; and several thousand individual pieces of ribbon. There is also a large collection of woven badges and labels. In addition The Herbert has various pieces of weaving machinery, of which the star item is a 19th century jacquard ribbon weaving loom.

The collection ranges in date from 1761 (the earliest ribbon in the collection, woven to celebrate the marriage of George III) to today. The largest group of ribbons, however, dates from the second half of the nineteenth century and contains many extraordinary and beautiful examples. Many are found pasted into sample books, which were ledgers full of short lengths of ribbon accumulated by a manufacturer or an individual weaver as a sales sample or a record of ribbons woven.

The uses to which ribbons were put were tremendously varied. As well as being attached to the body as dress trimmings, hat strings, shoes laces, sashes, belts, ties or braces, they were also to be found in the home as bellropes, furniture edging, curtain ties or fringes. They even appeared as upholstery edgings in horse-drawn and railway carriages.

Access to the Collection

A large part of the ribbon collection is housed in The Herbert's stores in order to preserve it. However it is possible to see the collection. If you are interested please contact the curatorial department at The Herbert. Details can be found on our website at www.theherbert.org.